NO GIRLS ALLOWED!

My book about me, my mates and God

Darren Hill and Alex Taylor

ISBN 978 1 84427 209 9

Scripture Union
207–209 Queensway, Bletchley, Milton Keynes MK2 2EB
Email: info@scriptureunion.org.uk

British Library Cataloguing-in-Publication Data.
A catalogue record of this book is available from the British Library.

Printed in India by Nutech Print Services India.

Cover and internal design: kwgraphicdesign

⎯ Scripture Union is an international Christian charity working with
churches in more than 130 countries.

Thank you for purchasing this book. Any profits from this book
support SU in England and Wales to bring the good news of Jesus
Christ to children, young people and families and to enable them to
meet God through the Bible and prayer.

Find out more about our work and how you can get involved at:
www.scriptureunion.org.uk (England and Wales)
www.suscotland.org.uk (Scotland)
www.suni.co.uk (Northern Ireland)
www.scriptureunion.org (USA)
www.su.org.au (Australia)

Contents

Welcome!

Welcome to _____

in the year 20_____ and Hi!

First let's say that this is YOUR book. Your book to enjoy and have fun with. Even better, you can make a record of what you're like now that will entertain you when you get old and wrinkly! We'll take a brief tour through the average life of a young lad – that's YOU if you weren't quite sure! Look at the Contents page and you'll find there's lots of stuff to interest and excite you. As you flick through the pages you'll learn more about yourself and the world you live in. By the end you'll hopefully know a little more about why you're here and what you can or should or could be doing. There's space for you to write and draw what you want, and extra pages at the back for you to write anything you want to remember.

So OK, with no more chat, let's get straight on and start the adventure called YOUR LIFE.

Alex Taylor is a fan of football, drama, singing and Fairly Odd Parents. He'd like to thank his own fairly odd parents and his housemates for hogging the TV so he could write his bits of the book! and

Darren Hill is just a guy who was once a boy but still likes to act like one! He'd like to thank Becki, Natasha, Jonathan and his mum and dad, and all the people at SU for their support and for not asking him to grow up!

Psst: Some answers are at the back but some answers are just upside down!

Yourself

You and your talents

This page is where it all starts. It's the place for you to say who you are and start to get to know yourself.

Challenge Put this book down and take a trip to the bathroom. Take a good long look at yourself in the mirror. Say "Hi".

You are a very special person! And you'll see as we go through **NO GIRLS ALLOWED!** that you are much, much, MUCH more than just what you saw in front of you in the mirror.

Challenge Go through these questions and gaps and fill them in.

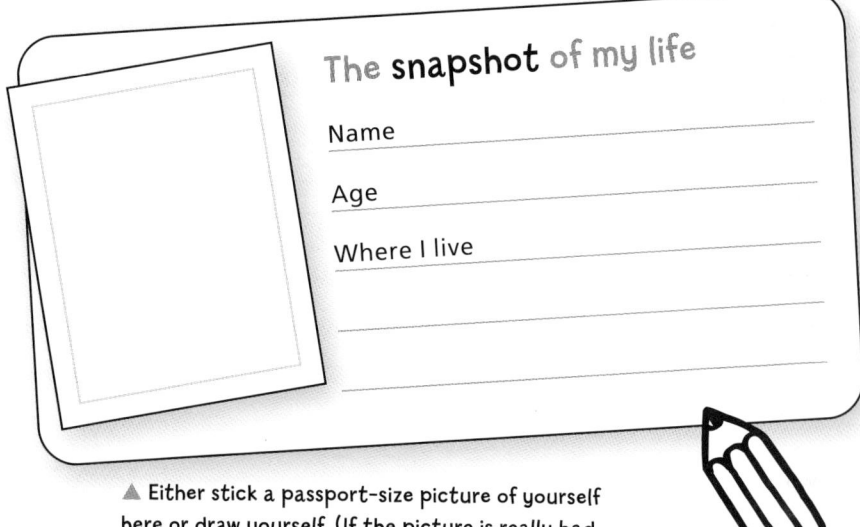

The snapshot of my life

Name _____

Age _____

Where I live _____

_____

_____

▲ Either stick a passport-size picture of yourself here or draw yourself. (If the picture is really bad you can always stick a photo over the top of it!)

What are you good at?

Circle some of the things, listed on the right, you think you can do well, or more importantly enjoy doing.

Look at things you've circled. Have you circled physical activities, or things that mean you can just sit down? Did you know sitting down all the time means we don't get to use our bodies to the max? Then again, if we don't use our brains fully, they are not being stre-e-e-etched and tuned up! So we need to try to get a healthy balance in our lives. Find a different colour pen and mark up any activities you'd like to do more of.

You are about to discover that you're a wonderful person, different to anyone else on the planet – good at some things and not so good at others. Thinking about all the stuff we like and don't like helps us to see who and what we are!

Feel free to write anything you want in this book. Make notes on the pages at the back to keep for the future.

In the years ahead you can pick up **NO GIRLS ALLOWED!** and see who

_____
(add your name)

aged _____ (add your age) **was.**

reading

writing

football

cricket

swimming

computer gaming

sleeping

eating

drawing

arguing

watching TV

watching films

talking

cooking

maths

history

music

running

tennis

basketball

rugby

taking care of pets…

Any other suggestions? Write here

_____

_____

_____

_____

_____

Psst: if you don't have a mirror in your bathroom, borrow one from a good friend. Or you could look at your reflection in a shop window. But don't get distracted by that new Wrestlemania game calling out to be bought!

Your self-image

On the last two pages you looked at who you are, what you like and what you could do more of. Now we'll look at how you feel about yourself.

Challenge Go through the following questions and answer them as honestly as you can with a tick or a cross. There are no right or wrong answers. We're all different.

□ **1** Do you like to be told when you've done something well?

□ **2** Do you enjoy being with your friends?

□ **3** Do you do your work at school confidently?

□ **4** Do you think you can do most things you try to do?

□ **5** Are you very good at all sports?

□ **6** Do you speak up at school when a question is asked?

□ **7** Do you like to win when you play games or sports?

□ **8** When asked to be at the front of the class to present something, do you look forward to it?

□ **9** Do you like to start conversations with someone else?

□ **10** Do you like answering these questions?

This is only a short list. If you ticked most of the questions, you are probably very confident. If you crossed most answers, then you may not feel so confident about yourself. It is possible to be too confident, or not confident enough. If you feel that you are one of these extremes you could look at ways of being different.

TOP TIPS

If we are **too confident** it is easy to stop caring about what we are doing and why we are doing it.

1 Think about whether you could use some help in doing something before rushing in.
2 Give someone else the chance to do something before you do.
3 We have TWO ears and only ONE mouth! Use them in that ratio. In other words, listen to others more than talking yourself!

If we are **not confident** enough we may not attempt to do things that we would be very good at.

1 Ask for help if you are not sure what you should be doing.
2 Attempt to do something without thinking about it – you may find it easier than you think.
3 It is OK to get things wrong or mess up – everyone does that at some point.

NEXT!

The **next** page may shine new light on you! And we'll come back to this on pages 76-79.

Your world

You and God

The Bible has a lot to say to us about who and what we are. It tells about why God made us, how he has helped the human race and what is going to happen in the future.

Challenge What do you think God thinks about you? Use the codecracker to work out some of the answers and then add your own ideas. Answers at the bottom of the page.

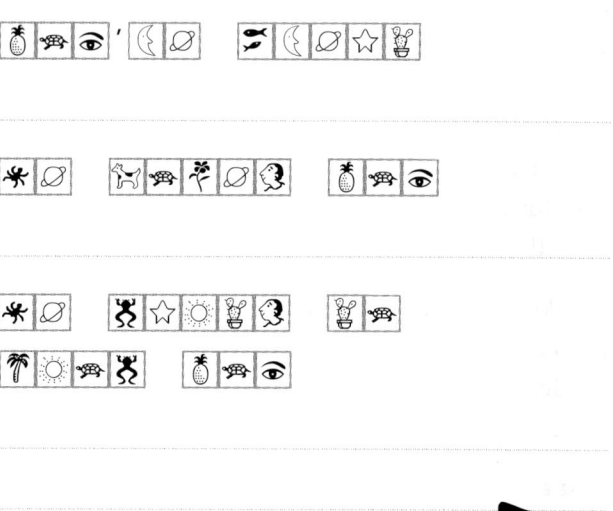

So, what does the Bible say about God and you?

God created us

In Genesis, the first book of the Bible, we read that God created everything there is – not just the earth, moon and sun, but everything – from the tiniest atom to the largest galaxy, even the human race!

God looked at what he had done. All of it was very good!

Genesis 1:31

God cares about us

God has given us the earth with all its richness – the sun and the rain to grow food, animals and birds to enjoy and care for, mountains and valleys for variety! And people to meet, know and love! God has given us everything we really need.

God wants us to be his friends

When God created the first human beings he wanted them to be his friends. But things began to go wrong very quickly and have been like that ever since. Look at the news to see just how bad things are. But the worst thing of all is that we turn away from the God who made us and loves us.

Look at the birds in the sky! They don't plant or harvest. They don't even store grain in barns. Yet your Father in heaven takes care of them. Aren't you worth more than birds?

Matthew 6:26

God knows that we're going to get things wrong, mess up and often forget about him. So he sent his son Jesus to help us become friends with God again. If we ask to be God's friend he won't turn us away.

You are unique

God wants to forgive us for the wrong things we do and help us to be different. Fancy being able to say that the Super-Being, who made everything there is, is your friend! Now that is truly amazing!

Even when we were God's enemies, he made peace with us, because his Son died for us.

Romans 5:10

U_ _ _ _ _

4,504 million km

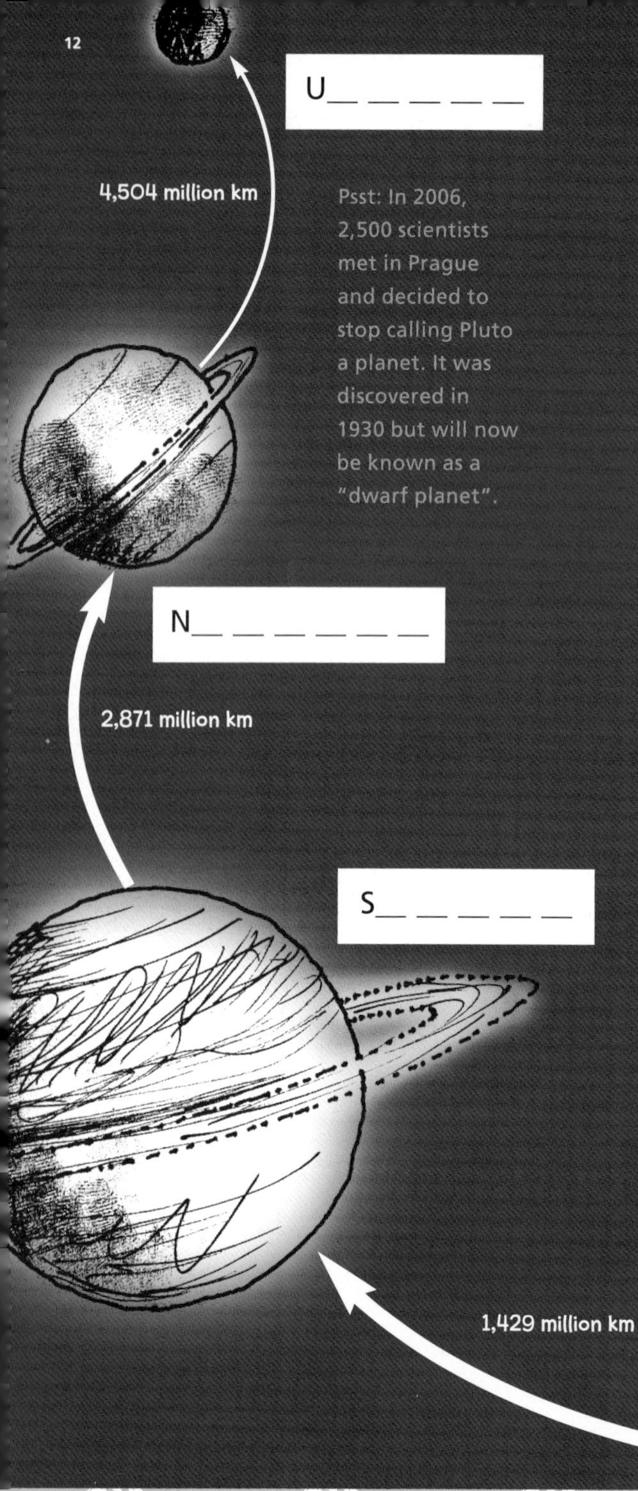

Psst: In 2006,
2,500 scientists
met in Prague
and decided to
stop calling Pluto
a planet. It was
discovered in
1930 but will now
be known as a
"dwarf planet".

N_ _ _ _ _ _

2,871 million km

S_ _ _ _ _

1,429 million km

Space

Have you ever stopped to think about how big the universe is? Stop what you're doing and think for a minute!

Imagine you've just grown a set of wings, or that you have just invented the best flying machine ever. You're flying up over your street, over your town, past other towns, cities, rivers, seas, oceans... You fly all around the world, getting back in time for your favourite TV programme. It's taken you about an hour to fly round the world (that's about 40,000 kilometres an hour!). If you flew at that speed, it would take you 9.5 hours to get to the moon, 1,950 hours to get to Mars. Keep going and in 15,700 hours you'll reach Jupiter. In 144,075 hours you'll reach Pluto. And even then you've only just travelled a fraction of the way across the universe.

Challenge Fill in the missing names of the planets. Answers at the bottom of the page.

Look up Psalm 33:6–9.

Ever wondered why the universe is so big?

55 million km

M_ _ _ _ _ _ _

108 million km

V_ _ _ _

150 million km

E_ _ _ _ _

228 million km

M_ _ _ _

778 million km

J_ _ _ _ _ _ _

Planet names: Mercury, Venus, Earth, Mars, Jupiter, Saturn, Neptune, Uranus

Calling Planet Earth...

Did you know that hundreds of years ago, people thought the earth was flat? They thought that if you went too far west across the ocean, you would fall off the edge!

We know that the earth is round, because we've seen pictures of it from space.

So that's what the earth looks like from above. But what about from below? Here is a cutaway picture of the earth. It has layers, a bit like an onion (but it doesn't make your eyes water).

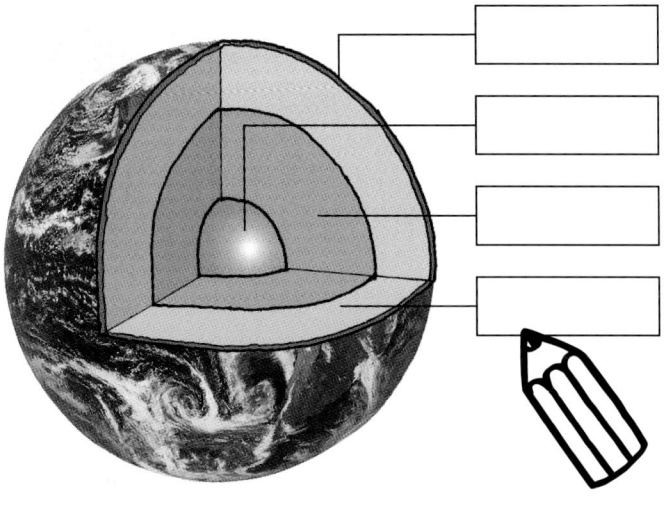

Challenge Find out what all these layers are called. Look on the Internet or in a book at the library.

Some people have tried to imagine what it must be like. A man called Jules Verne wrote a book called *Journey to the Centre of the Earth*. If you like reading, find a copy to see what he imagined.

Challenge The things that Isaac Newton came up with were really scientific, but you can do an experiment a bit like the falling apple. Turn to pages 18 and 19!

Lots of animals

How many animals are mentioned in the Bible? Do you know?

Challenge Make a list of all the animals in the Bible you can remember. Or, you could even have a competition with a friend! How many can you remember in 60 seconds?

Animals in the Bible

....

....

....

....

....

....

....

....

....

....

....

....

....

....

....

....

....

How many animals has God created? Only God knows. There are hundreds of thousands of different species in existence and explorers and scientists are still finding more!

Where are some, but there are loads more: donkeys, pigs, doves, sheep, dogs, goats, ravens, cows, lions, horses, even something called a behemoth. This could have been a hippopotamus, but no one is quite sure – check out Job 40:15–24.

God said, "Now we will make humans, and they will be like us. We will let them rule the fish, the birds, and all other living creatures."

Genesis 1:26

BODY of a cheetah

LEG of a starfish

WING of an eagle

EYE of a fly

LOSE a mouth or beak

BODY of a kangaroo

START

FIN of a shark

LOSE an eye

BEAK of a toucan

HEAD of a goose

Challenge Create some animals yourself! Try this game with one or more of your friends.

LOSE a leg, wing or fin

LOSE a head

You'll each need:
- a counter
- a pencil
- a sheet of paper
- one dice

You need to collect:
- 1 body
- 4 legs, wings or fins
- 1 mouth or beak
- 1 head
- 2 eyes

HEAD of a gorilla

EYE of a cat

EYE of an owl

WING of a parrot

Throw the dice and move around the board. When you land on a square, draw that animal part on your paper. If you lose a part, rub it out! At the end of the game, you will all have drawn some rather strange animals! Take a look at the animals your mates have created.

LOSE a body

LEG of an octopus

MOUTH of a donkey

EYE of a snail

MOUTH of a bear

BODY of an eel

HEAD of a penguin

LOSE a leg, wing or fin

LEG of a giraffe

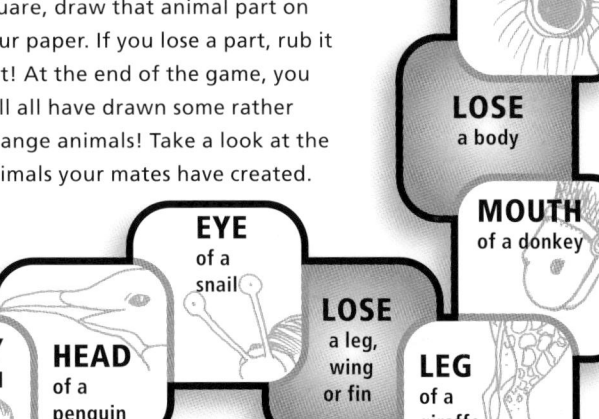
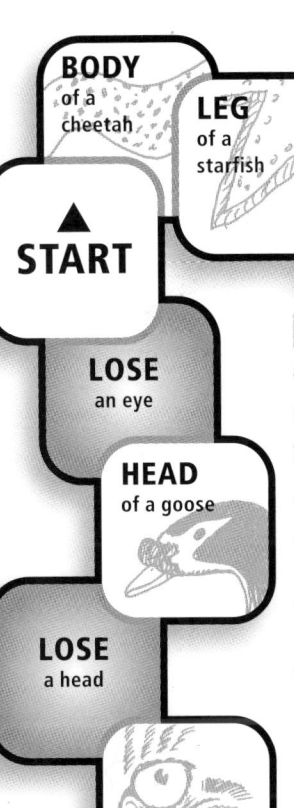

Your head

Experiments

We all fall down!

Challenge Collect a few objects of different weights, such as a feather, a ping-pong ball, a tennis ball, a book or a piece of paper. Find a non-wobbly chair, not too high, and stand on it. (Don't fall off!)

What you do:
- Drop your objects one by one to the floor.
- Get a friend to watch how they drop – do they fall straight to the floor? Does one object fall more quickly than all the others? Why is this?
- Predict how things are going to fall before you drop them.
- Write up your results below.

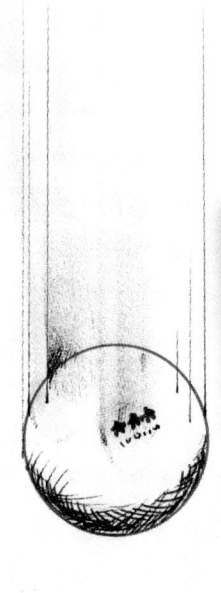

Item	Time

left little finger

right little finger

left ring finger

right ring finger

left middle finger

right middle finger

left index finger

right index finger

left thumb

right thumb

Fingerprints

God made us all different, and that includes our fingerprints! So each one of your fingers and thumbs has a unique pattern on it – how amazing is that?

Challenge **See how different your fingerprints are.**

What you do:

- Get an ink pad (make sure it's not a permanent ink pad).
- Press each of your fingers onto the pad and then press them onto the boxes. Can you see how different they are? Check out a mate's prints and see how unique you are!

Cola corrosion!

Challenge **See how destructive cola can be!**

What you do:

- Take four glasses of cola and put one of the following things (or something similar) in each glass, depending on what you have available: a penny or a nail, a piece of cooked ham, a piece of banana, a match.
- Put the same items in four glasses of water.
- For the next four days, see how much of each item in the cola is left. Compare with the stuff in the water.

Are you surprised what cola can do?

Puzzles

Maths puzzles

Your brain is amazing. It can do any number of things as it learns.

Challenge How many squares can you find in the following image?

Check the answers at the back of the book, page 95!

"I can read your mind!"

Challenge Try this on your friends! They'll think you can read their minds!

Think of a number between two and ten

times it by two

add two

take away four

add seven

subtract five

divide by the number you first thought of

and your answer will be

"TWO"

Numbers in words

Challenge Write one to ten in different languages.

Not the numbers 1,2,3, but the words! How many languages do you and your school friends know?

If you can, write the numbers down as words. Do you see any similarities between the words? Do any of them sound similar to English?

Logic puzzles

Maths puzzles use the special "numbers" part of your brain. But your brain can do a whole lot more than juggle with numbers. Sometimes it is more logical to make connections between the things you see. These puzzles are designed to challenge your brain to make the connections.

Challenge What are the missing letters in the following sequence?

Check the answer at the back of the book, page 95!

J F M A M _ _ A S _ N D

Challenge Look at this grid and see if you can do what is written below.

Starting anywhere on the grid you need to draw a straight line that passes through all the dots on the grid. You can only change direction three times, and the line must remain straight.

Check the answer at the back of the book, page 95!

Challenge What word is missing from this list?

Check the answer at the back of the book, page 95!

Sneezy
Doc
Grumpy
Happy
Bashful
Dopey

Making connections and using the "logic" side of our brains has helped humans learn more about the world they live in. We've learned how the body works to find cures for illnesses and how the world's weather systems work to forecast tornadoes and hurricanes (although mistakes are made!). If YOU can use this skill you never know what discoveries and connections YOU could make!

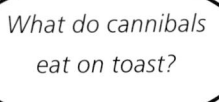
What do cannibals eat on toast?

Baked Beings!

What do you call a bad lion tamer?

Claude Bottom!

Word puzzles

Poetry helps to improve your word power. The poet can express ideas and stories in word pictures. The book of Psalms in the middle of the Bible is written in poetic language. Some of the psalms are written in the form of "acrostic" poetry where each line begins with the next letter of the alphabet (it's said ak-ross-tik).

Challenge **Write an acrostic poem where each line begins with a letter of your name.**

The poem could be about yourself or God.

Challenge What words fill in the blank to make two new words?

B A C K __ __ __ __ A G E

H U M A N __ __ __ __ N E S S

F O O T __ __ __ __ F A S T

Check the answers at the back of the book, page 95!

Challenge Wordsearching

The 13 words on the right were placed into the puzzle. Can you find them all?

G	U	S	V	I	Q	I	L	K	A	R	T
R	S	W	Y	D	E	W	O	L	L	A	0
G	J	C	N	O	O	O	B	P	E	J	B
B	Y	Q	N	G	B	Q	U	R	X	M	E
T	M	G	I	P	K	R	R	M	Z	L	S
O	D	I	A	X	Q	D	L	B	C	A	C
N	E	R	R	A	D	N	P	E	D	K	Q
S	C	L	B	M	C	V	L	X	R	Z	L
S	S	S	C	E	A	Z	K	L	L	J	O
F	F	U	T	S	A	Q	F	C	O	U	T
R	K	X	W	K	U	N	C	V	T	P	I
V	Z	O	A	I	F	M	B	G	V	L	K

ALEX
ALLOWED
ART
BOYS
BRAIN
DARREN
GIRLS
GOD
MUSCLE
SCRAPBOOK
SMELL
SNOT
STUFF

Check the answer at the back of the book, page 95!

Spot the difference

Can you find the **10** differences in these two pictures?

Check the answers at the back of the book, page 95!

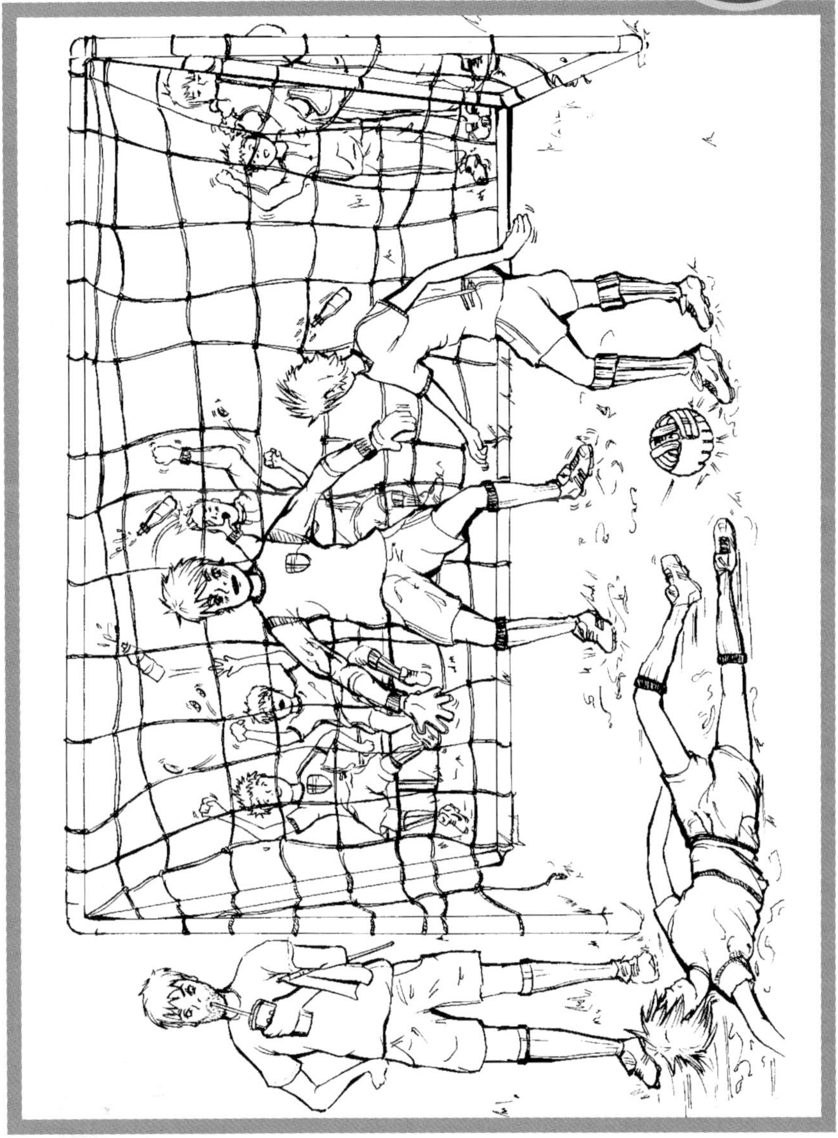

Quiz time

Challenge How much do you really know about this wonderful world you live in? Here's a fantastic quiz for you to try. The answers are on page 31 – and no cheating!

Put a tick or cross in the box when you check the answer

1 Which is the biggest land animal?

2 What is the world's biggest ocean?

3 How many hours are there in a day?

4 Which is the world's highest mountain?

5 Which is the largest bird?

6 What grows in paddy fields?

7 What does a caterpillar turn into?

8 Is the spider an insect?

9 Which parts of the earth have the longest summer days?

10 Which is the world's biggest desert?

11 Which vegetable has a big orange-red root?

12 In which town was Jesus born?

13 You can see through it and it is made of sand. What is it?

14 What is kelp?

15 Which American animal sprays a foul-smelling liquid to defend itself?

16 What happens to your eyes when you sneeze?

17 Which letter begins the fewest English words?

18 What is the Great Barrier Reef in Australia made from?

19 What is the most common disease?

20 Cream, butter, cheese and yogurt are all made of what?

21 Which sea lies between Africa and Europe?

22 Iceberg and cos are types of what?

23 What is the plural of sheep?

24 How deep is the deepest part of the ocean: 1.6, 4.8 or 11.2 kilometres?

25 What divides the northern and the southern hemisphere?

26 What causes tides?

27 How does a marsupial carry its young?

28 On which tree do acorns grow?

29 Which animal has the longest nose?

30 What is chlorophyll?

So... how did you do?

Don't worry if you didn't do as well as you thought. One of the amazing things about us is that we learn as we grow. If you tried this quiz again in six months time, you'd do much better. Anyway for all your effort, whether you didn't do too well or if you got top marks, here is a prize! 👉

Answers

1 African elephant
2 The Pacific
3 24
4 Everest 8,848 m
5 The ostrich
6 Rice
7 A butterfly or moth
8 No (insects have 6 legs and a spider has 8)
9 The North Pole and the South Pole
10 The Sahara in Africa
11 The carrot
12 Bethlehem
13 Glass
14 Seaweed
15 Skunk
16 They close
17 X
18 Coral
19 The common cold
20 Milk
21 The Mediterranean
22 Lettuce
23 Sheep
24 11.2 kilometres
25 The equator
26 The pull of the moon
27 In its pouch
28 Oak
29 The elephant (its trunk)
30 A green substance that enables growth, found in plants

Your whole body

Sport

Extreme sports

"LIVE LIFE TO THE MAX"
"IN YER FACE"
"Let's get ready to rumble"

These are all phrases used in sports that are taking the world by storm. In recent years the traditional sports of football, rugby, skiing and so on have been seen by some as a little tame. So the concept of extreme sports was born.

It started off, for example, with…

Skateboarding

BMX bike riding

Snowboarding

…but soon increased to other extreme ideas such as

Base jumping

Bungee jumping

White-water rafting

And recently new extremes have been tried. Someone has even done extreme ironing, skydiving with an ironing board!

Psst: We are not giving you permission to do something dangerous! You'll have to ask someone responsible for you about that!

Why do we get excited about extreme forms of sports? Here are a few suggestions:

1 Life can sometimes be a little boring and dull. We need some excitement!

2 We have most things we need. OK, there is plenty to worry about (like what's happening at school, at home and so on) but most readers of **NO GIRLS ALLOWED!** don't have the kind of worries that people in the Third World have. (Like, for example, where our next meal is coming from or whether we'll be able to get some good medicine.) So we can spend more time thinking about crazy stuff like extreme sports...

3 We have always needed adrenalin to find food. Although a trip to the supermarket can be filled with danger (being hit by a wandering trolley), it isn't the same as having to hunt and grow your own food. There is adrenalin going spare for dangerous (and fun) sports like this!

But don't forget that God wants us to look after our bodies!

Our lives are a gift from him. There is nothing wrong with excitement but, if we hurt ourselves, there won't be much excitement for a long time afterwards!

Winning and losing

We all like to win. If someone wins, someone else loses. When we win we feel very happy, but when we lose we may feel upset. The secret is to enjoy sports whatever the result.

When we win it's OK to be pleased but it's not always helpful to go over the top! We need to learn to be humble when we win (that means, not having too big an idea of ourselves!). Then again, when we lose we should be satisfied with what we've done. Maybe this time we were beaten by someone better. Maybe we need to practise more or not get distracted. Maybe we're just not that good! We need to learn to lose with dignity! You'll probably already know that being humble is easier said than done.

Challenge **Imagine you score the winning goal. What might you feel?** Answers at the bottom of the page.

Anything else?

The best example of someone being humble is Jesus. He had the strength and power to do anything, as he was God's Son. But he didn't use that power to show off. Instead he put it all to one side when he came from heaven to earth. Look at the verse on the right to see how the Bible puts it.

Remember – all our abilities and gifts come from God. So when you play hard and win, thank God for those abilities.

But what about if we lose?

Challenge **How would you feel if you missed a penalty in a penalty shoot-out?** Answers at the bottom of the page.

Anything else?

There is usually another opportunity. If we have tried our best, we can do no more. And if we were not trying, there is something to learn from this. God knows how we feel. As the Bible puts it:

God cares for you, so turn all your worries over to him.

1 Peter 5:7

Christ was truly God. But he did not try to remain equal with God. Instead he gave up everything and became a slave, when he became like one of us. Christ was humble. He obeyed God and even died on a cross.

Philippians 2:6–8

DID YOU KNOW?

...that Jesus was God in a body? He came to earth so that we could be friends with God. And he also came to show us what God is like.

SICK, GUTTED, DISAPPOINTED

Teamwork

Challenge What sports can you do on your own?
Answers at the bottom of the page.

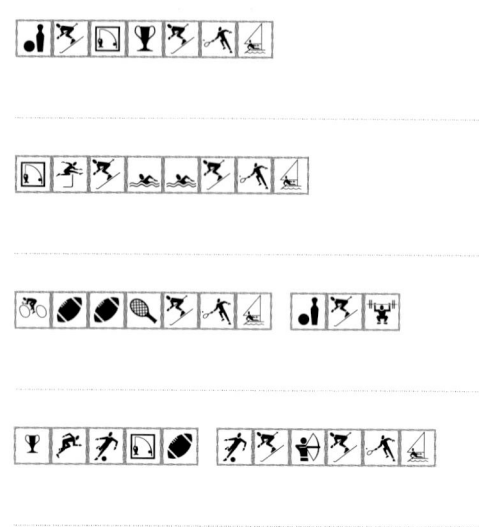

Add any others you can think of.

Most sports mean you have to join in with others in some way!

Challenge Write the name of your favourite team on this scarf.

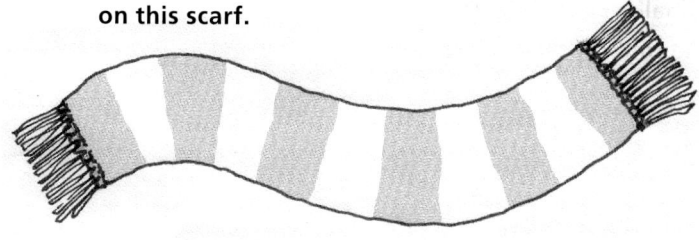

FISHING, SWIMMING, KEEPING FIT, HORSE RIDING

Being part of a team is fun and challenging. Most teams we think of are sports teams. And because we're in the sports section of NO GIRLS ALLOWED! that's our main focus. But we could be talking about any time you need to work with other people.

Challenge Think of times you work with other people. Make a list here.

The most successful teams are ones that work well together. Can you remember when a football team in a lower league beat a superstarred team from the Premiership? This probably happened because on that particular day the less famous side played better together, as a team, than the others did.

Jesus knew the importance of working as a team. He chose 12 people to be in his team. They were called the disciples and when he asked them to do something for the first time they didn't go out on their own. He sent them in pairs, their own little teams.

Challenge Check out Mark 6:7-11 to find out what he told these little teams to do!

Comedy sport?

God doesn't want us to be boring and dull! He wants us to be happy, so let's have a little laugh.

In 2005 many people in England went mad with cricket fever when England played five matches against Australia for the Ashes (some burnt cricket stumps in a little pot!). Australian cricketers tend to win more matches and be more passionate about the game. However, that year, England had a team that could win and they did. The country had some new national heroes!

Challenge **How much do you know about cricket? Look at the list below to spot the made-up cricket positions, which you wouldn't find on the cricket field. There are 11!**

OWZAT!

- ☐ Silly mid-on
- ☐ Silly mid-leg
- ☐ Short extra-cover
- ☐ Long backward-cover
- ☐ Long leg
- ☐ Short leg
- ☐ Middle leg
- ☐ Backward square point
- ☐ Forward round spike
- ☐ Long off
- ☐ Way long off

- ☐ Fine leg
- ☐ Bad leg
- ☐ Gully
- ☐ Wally
- ☐ Mid-on
- ☐ Right on
- ☐ Right off
- ☐ First slip
- ☐ Last slip
- ☐ Slip up
- ☐ Wicket keeper

Check the answers at the back of the book, pages 94–95!

It is a funny game with some strange rules and even stranger positions. Not as simple as football or rugby with its forwards, backs and goalkeepers.

Sports we wish we could play

There is an almost endless list of sports to be played or watched. Here are some sports that have so far not been played but which would be lots of fun to watch. Can you think of any others to add?

Indoor yachting

Deep-sea horse racing

Underwater diving

Desert water polo

Table rugby

Slug football

Shopping basketball

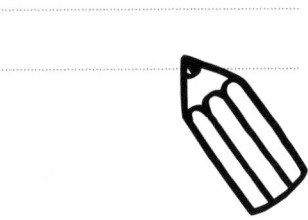

Dance

Now, I know what you're thinking. Dance? Are you sure? Well, yes! Why not give it a go? Dancing is a way you can use your body to say things that you might not be able to say with words.

Challenge What kinds of dancing do you know about?

Answers at the bottom of the page 41.

Can you think of any more dances?

Challenge Have a go at dancing yourself. You don't have to have gone to ballet lessons, or learnt how to tap dance – anyone can do it!

Step-by-step guide to start dancing

1 Find a picture that has lots of people in it and choose one of them.

2 What do you think they are like? Do they look happy? Sad? Angry? Decide how they feel and think about how they would walk.

3 Practise walking up and down, pretending to be that person. If you think they are sad, you might walk slowly, dragging your feet along the floor and frowning. If you think they are excited, you might jump and leap around.

4 Find a piece of music that matches the feelings of your person and walk around to the music.

5 If you're doing this with someone else, what would your characters do if they met each other?

David, a famous king from the Bible, danced in front of everyone, even though he was a big strong king. He wanted to say something, but didn't know the words to use. He was talking to God.

Challenge **Want to find out more? Read the story in the Bible in 2 Samuel 6:1–19.**

What do you think David was feeling? Was he happy? Excited? Angry?

YOU can talk to God just like David did! You can tell God how you are feeling without using words. You can use your movements instead. For example, if you're feeling sad, put some sad music on, and walk around in a sad way. God will understand what you are telling him!

God made snot!

Yes, he did! Snot is one of the many important ways our body keeps healthy, so let's take a closer look. No, I don't mean putting something you picked from your own nose under a microscope, but...

Challenge **Have a feel of your nose. Wiggle it, stroke it, bend the edges, twist it round, try to touch the tip with your tongue!**

Look at your nose closely in the mirror. Move it around. Is it straight or hooked? Have you got big nostrils or little ones, hairy ones or smooth ones?

Noses are for making sure that air gets into the body and goes down into the lungs. These take important things out of the air (like oxygen) and pass them around to the rest of the body, to keep the body going. A maze of bones and wiggles make sure the air passes through lots of snot, to clean and warm it. Snot is also slightly antiseptic, which means it fights and kills germs itself!

Want to find out more? Read *God Made Snot* by Matt Campbell.

A gloopy book of facts about snot: where it's from, why we have it and what God's got to do with it!

£4.99 (price correct at the time of going to print)

Psst: Turn to page 56 to find out more about smelling!

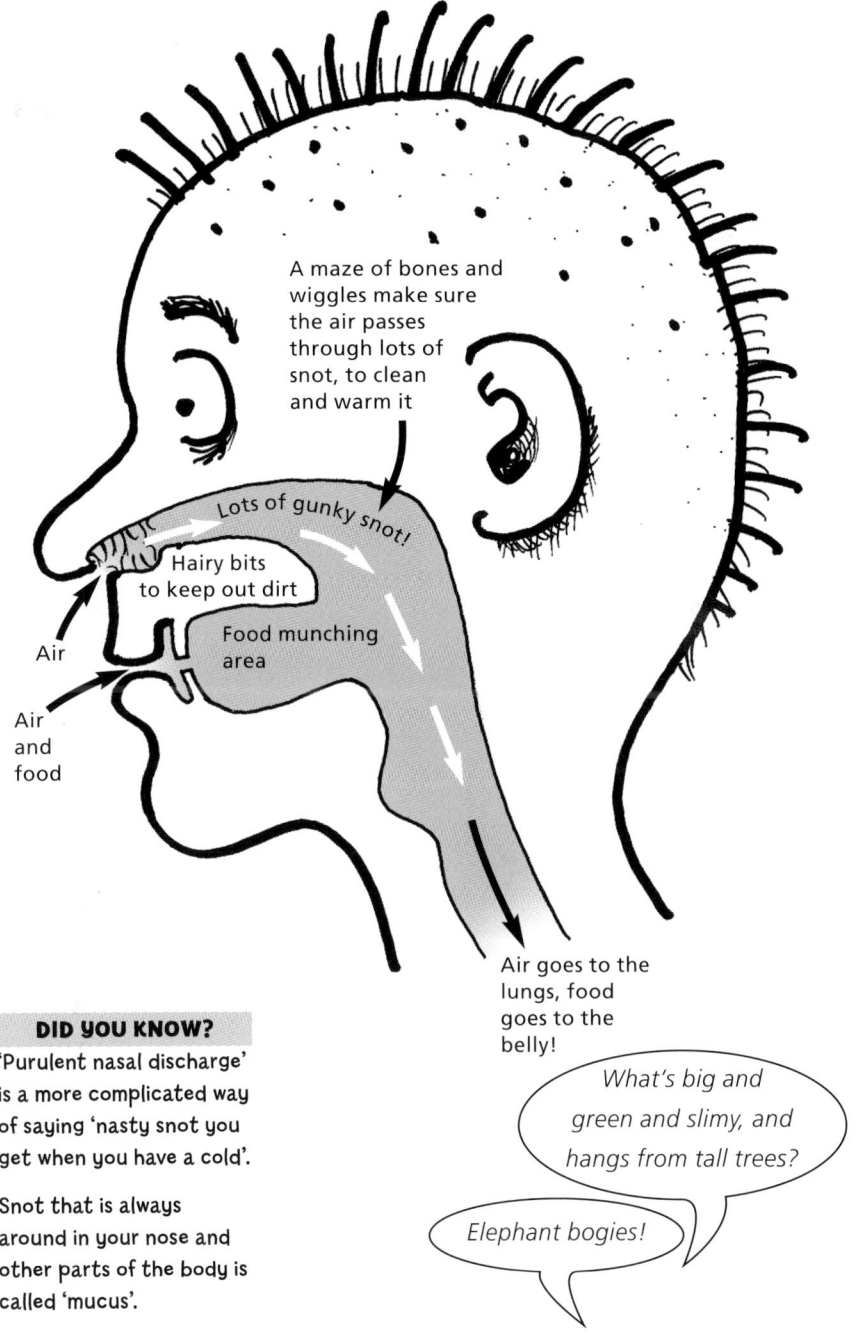

A maze of bones and wiggles make sure the air passes through lots of snot, to clean and warm it

Lots of gunky snot!

Hairy bits to keep out dirt

Food munching area

Air

Air and food

Air goes to the lungs, food goes to the belly!

DID YOU KNOW?

'Purulent nasal discharge' is a more complicated way of saying 'nasty snot you get when you have a cold'.

Snot that is always around in your nose and other parts of the body is called 'mucus'.

What's big and green and slimy, and hangs from tall trees?

Elephant bogies!

Bony stuff

God made skulls and skeletons to help us stand up!
Imagine if you had no bones in your body – what
would you look like?

Challenge Draw a picture of someone with no
bones!

Challenge Find out the names for some of the
bones in your body.

M ....

C ....

S ....

R ....

H ....

F ....

P ....

T ....

M ....

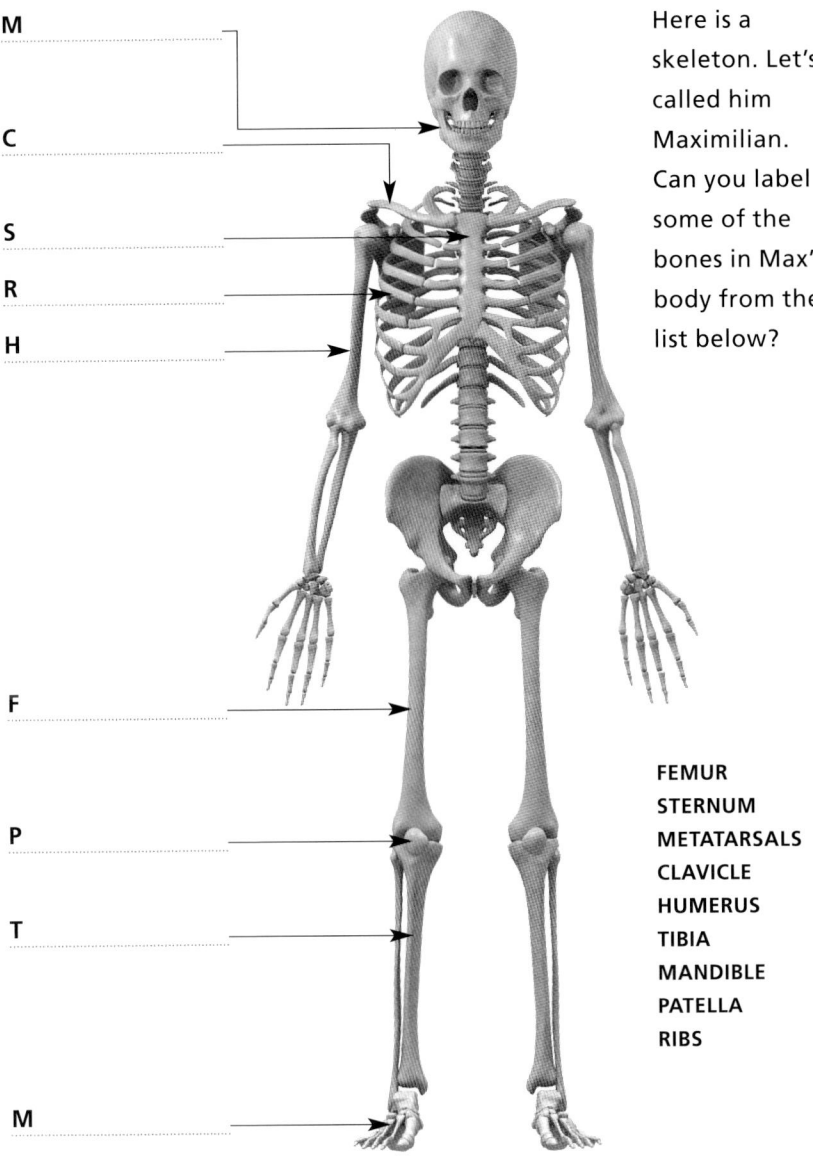

Here is a skeleton. Let's called him Maximilian. Can you label some of the bones in Max's body from the list below?

FEMUR
STERNUM
METATARSALS
CLAVICLE
HUMERUS
TIBIA
MANDIBLE
PATELLA
RIBS

Challenge Can you feel some of the bones in your own body? You should be able to feel your ribs, kneecaps, shoulder blades – even your ankles!

Your hands

Be crafty

Origami is the art of folding paper. You can make some great models from folding just one piece of paper. Go online or get down to your library to find out more! For now, is a "birdy" model for you to make!

Challenge

Make a pecking pigeon

This is a really easy one to get you started!

1 Take a square of paper and fold it in half from corner to corner. Open it out again.

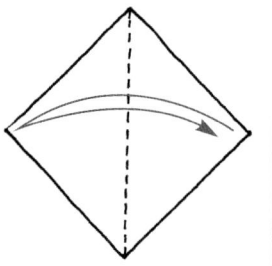

2 From the top point, fold the sloping sides so that they meet along the centre fold line.

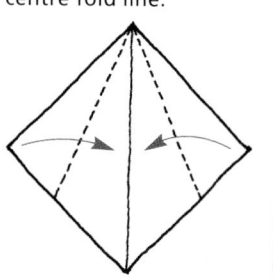

3 You should have a kite shape. Fold this in half along your first fold line.

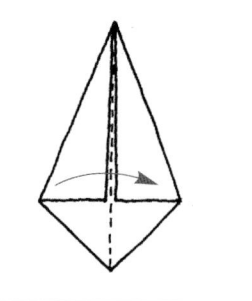

4 Turn the paper round and fold the thinnest point down. Unfold it again.

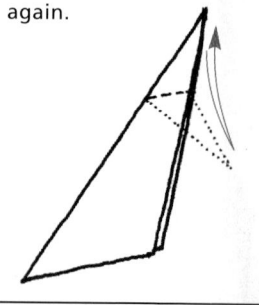

5 Now fold the point the other way along the same fold line. Unfold it again.

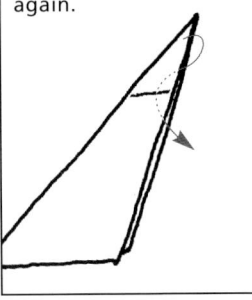

6 Following the fold lines you made in 4 and 5, push the point down inside the model, so that you form the beak of the pigeon.

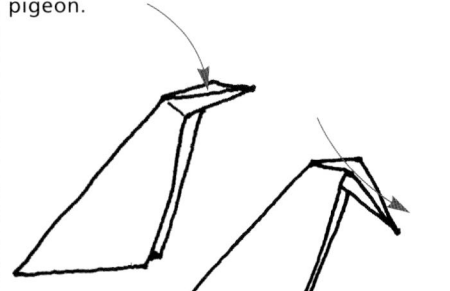

7 To make the pigeon peck, push its tail down and let go!

Art!

Another way to use your hands is to create a picture. What's the most beautiful thing you can think of?

Challenge **Paint a peacock picture**

All you have to do:

Get several different colours of runny poster or powder paint (especially shades of blue) and carefully put them onto paper plates. Make sure you cover the table with newspaper or an old sheet. Put your thumb in the paint and create feather shapes to make the fantail of this peacock

Alternatively, enlarge and copy this drawing of the peacock's body onto a large piece of paper. Making sure you are wearing old clothes and the floor is well covered, put your hand in the paint, then press it onto the paper to make handprint feathers for the fantail. Keep going until you have a magnificent peacock!

You can get finger-paint from many shops – it's thinner than ordinary paint, so doesn't go everywhere when you use it! What kind of things can you paint using your fingerprints? Use this space here to experiment!

Did you hear the story about the peacock?

No? I heard it's a wonderful tale!

Cartoon time

Ever wanted to draw cartoons really, really well?

Ever started to draw something, hoping it would look like SpongeBob SquarePants or Fairly Odd Parents, but then found that the finished picture looked a bit as if your auntie had sat on it for a whole day?

Here are some great tips to help you start to draw cartoons.

How to draw people

1 Rough pencil sketch...   **2** Add some detail...   **3** Finish off with a felt pen

Some facial expressions...

Hair and heads...

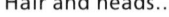

Cartoon stories

Now you've started to draw characters, put them in a story. Think of a short event that could happen to one of your characters. Then try and split it into four parts. These are going to be your four pictures.

Here's an idea to start you off.

1 A man walks along a street. A woman walks towards him.

2 Same man in same street. First woman almost out of sight. Identical woman walks towards him. Puzzled man.

3 Same man. Second woman almost out of sight. Identical woman walks towards him. Very puzzled man.

4 Man turns around to see triplets.

1

2

3

4

Tell us a story!

What kind of stories do you like to read? What's your favourite story?

Challenge Finish this story yourself. Decide what happens to the characters! What do they say? What do they do? If you don't like how it ends, rub it out and start again! This story starts off being based on the story of the Good Samaritan (look it up in Luke 10:25–37) but you can make whatever you want happen!

One day, Josh was walking down the road, wearing his new Manchester United shirt. It was bright red and had the name of his favourite player on the back. As he passed a shop window he looked at his reflection. He looked good! He stood there for a moment, and started to daydream. He was walking out of the players' tunnel at old Trafford. The crowd roared as he jogged onto the pitch and some of them were even chanting his name! He smiled.

"Look, he's laughing at his own reflection!" said a voice behind him. Josh turned around, his thoughts still on the green grass of old Trafford. He was shocked to see four lads, older than him, all wearing sky-blue Manchester City shirts.

"Get him, lads!" shouted one of them and they pushed him to the ground.

After a while, they walked off, shouting, "Now who's the best football team?" Josh lay on the ground, groaning. He hurt all over and couldn't move. He couldn't see anyone around to help him. His shirt was ripped. He began to cry. What was he going to do?

Just then, a big black car drove up and stopped by the side of him. The window opened and Josh was surprised to see...

Who (or what) was Josh surprised to see? How does the story end? You decide!

Write down any ideas of what could happen. You might get your mates to help you decide. Then choose the best idea and write an ending for the story. Was your ending like the one in the Bible story? If so, why? If not, why not? What do other people think of your story? Read it to them and find out!

Other hobbies

Each to their own!

What hobbies do you have? Are you an accomplished philatelist? (That's a stamp collector!) Or are you a keen campanologist? (A bell-ringer, if you didn't know!) Here's our handy guide to some hobbies you might not have tried!

Stamp collecting

Every country in the world produces stamps. And people collect them and stick them in books.

The most expensive stamp ever is a Swedish stamp dating from 1855. In 2003, someone paid $2,240,000 (that's about £1,190,000) for it. It is so valuable because it is the only one in the world.

To find out more, check out these websites:
- www.coins.about.com
- www.stampsales.com
- www.gibbonsstampmonthly.com

DID YOU KNOW?

The first stamp was produced in Britain and introduced on 6 May 1840. It was called the Penny Black and is one of the most expensive stamps to add to your collection.

Chess

Chess is played between two players using a board made up of 64 black and white squares. Each player has 16 pieces, which move across the board in different directions and have strange names. Kings, queens and knights fight against bishops, rooks and pawns.

There are world championships, national tournaments and local competitions. Anyone can play! You just need to learn the rules. Chess sets are very cheap, so once you get the rules in your head

A WACKY CHESS FACT

Chess is believed to have originated in India in the sixth Century! It was called Chaturanga.

and the pieces in your hand, all you need is a mate to play against!

To find out more, check out this website to find a local chess club. They have details of many junior chess clubs – www.bcf.org.uk

Fishing

Ever fancied sitting by a river in the rain for hours on end? It's not everyone's idea of a great time! But, thousands of people love to go down to the waterside to see if they can catch some fish.

Here is what Matt, a keen fisherman, says: "I like fishing because it's full of surprises. You glimpse a flash of silver near your line – is it a minnow? Is it a monster? Has it seen the hook? Will it take the bait? Your heart starts pounding, your palm gets sweaty and your arm gets an attack of the twitches. You've got to have the reactions of a cat – and so you sit and wait... And you do this in the long, hot summer and in the frozen depths of winter – just for that moment, that rush of adrenaline. Is it a minnow? Is it a monster?"

A rod, line, bait and hook are the essential things you need, and maybe lots of food to keep you going! But you can get a lot more kit to go with it!

If you're serious about finding out more about fishing, then check out these websites. They have details of clubs in the UK!
• www.go-fishing.co.uk
• www.fishing4fun.co.uk
• www.maggotdrowning.com

A WACKY FISHING FACT

The largest fish caught in the world is a white shark, caught off the Australian coast in 1959. It weighed 1,208 kg.

All website addresses are correct at time of going to press.

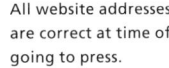

Your senses

Your nose

What's the very worst smell you can think of – even worse than your Uncle Frank's shoes, or the smell of your PE kit after it's been left in a bag for three weeks?

My worst smell is

....

What's the very best smell you've ever smelt – better than hot chocolate or the best pizza in the world?

My best smell is

....

Challenge **Test your friends' noses!**

What you do:

Get together some stuff that's really smelly – for this, you may need the help of your mum or dad or whoever looks after you. Collect things you might have around the house, such as onions, cinnamon sticks, vinegar or cola. DON'T get anything that is powdery (like ground pepper or flour that might make your friends sneeze really badly!) or anything that is a chemical (like cleaning liquid, bleach or anything you can't get the lid off!).

Put all your smells into containers with lids on. Blindfold your friends one at a time. Get them to smell your smelly stuff and record what they think it is.

Friend's name		Friend's name	
What they think the smell is	**What the smell really is**	What they think the smell is	**What the smell really is**

It's amazing how you can tell what something is by the smell. Our noses are GREAT! To see how your nose works sometimes, look at pages 42 and 43 – it's all about snot!

God made us individually. He made our noses and the way we smell. We're going to think about other amazing ways God made for us to explore the world around us in the next few pages, as we look at more of our senses.

Nothing about me is hidden from you!
I was secretly woven together
deep in the earth below,
but with your own eyes
you saw my body being formed.

Psalm 139:15–16

Why are giraffes' necks so long?

Because their feet stink!

Your eyes

Read this!

Do you like reading? If you do, you'll know that books open up a whole new world of imagination and experiences. Earlier, we asked you about what kind of stories you like to read, and your favourite story. What's your favourite book? And why?

Challenge Find out what other people like to read. Does your sister enjoy *Harry Potter*? Is your friend's best read *Wolf Brother*?

Who	Favourite book	Why?

Challenge Go into your library and see what new books are there.

Are there more story books, information books, picture books or joke books? Ask the person in charge of the library how they decide what new books to buy.

Are you a member of a library? Libraries are fantastic places where you can read all the latest books FREE! Yes, that's right, FREE! All you have to do is join. Take your mum or dad or whoever looks after you with you to the library and one of the librarians will make sure you do everything you need to get a library card. Then you can take out books for three weeks at a time – more than enough to read and enjoy the latest stories!

What do you call a deer with no eyes?

No idea!

What do you call a deer with no eyes and no legs?

Still no idea!

Do you read the Bible at all? Reading the Bible helps you know more about Jesus. There's a story about a man called Philip. To his surprise he found himself in the desert when a chariot whizzed past him. Inside this chariot was a rich, powerful, black man who was trying to read part of the Old Testament, the first part of the Bible. But he couldn't make sense of it even though he could read. God told Philip to run really fast to catch up with the chariot and offer to help this man understand.

The man was reading how Jesus came to earth and died which was all part of God's big plan. He didn't know much about Jesus. He needed Philip to explain. You can read this story in Acts 8:26–40.

You may find reading the Bible a bit hard. Ask someone to help you, just as Philip helped this powerful man. Or maybe *Snapshots* can help. *Snapshots* comes out every three months with a bit of Bible to read, puzzles, prayer suggestions and info. It helps people your age get to know God better through reading the Bible and talking with God. Available from all good Christian bookshops.

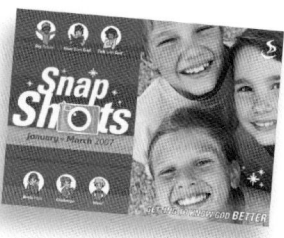

Your ears

Music!

Ever wondered why there are so many different styles of music? You might think that what you like is good music, and every other style is just rubbish (well, do you? Be honest!).

Challenge **Find some music that other people like, but you don't, and listen to it!**

This might be a CD of your mum's (maybe Abba, opera or classical music!) or something your granny enjoys (could be Tom Jones or Cliff Richard!). Listen, and then fill in this table. Or, if you can't stand the idea of doing that, get together with your mates and listen to some of their music. See if you can all fill in the table. Think hard – can you find anything

Whose music	Good points

about the song/music that is good? Put it into the
"Good points" column. Put all the stuff you don't
like about it into the "Bad points" column. What
are the words like? Do they make sense? Are they
all slushy and about love? Write it down in the
"Mad words" column. After the song has finished,
have you changed your mind about whether you
like it? Write "yes" or "no" in the "Do you like it?"
column!

What does all this different music mean? We all
have different tastes, we all like listening to
different things. God makes each one of us with a
different character, different likes and dislikes. How
boring would it be if we were all the same? What
would it be like if we all liked Cliff Richard or Abba?

Bad points	Mad words	Do you like it?

Playing music

Challenge Find out how many different musical instruments your family and friends play.

You may have had the chance to learn a musical instrument already. But as you get older, you may be able to learn more. Most secondary schools offer a choice of lessons from a wide variety of instruments. Maybe your primary school does too!

Here is something about a few instruments you might come across:

Wind for example – flute
This is played by blowing over a hole at one end. You close holes further down the flute to change the note you make.

String for example – violin
You play it by holding one end under your chin and moving a bow back and forth over the strings above a hole in the middle. To change a note you press a string down in different positions on the neck of the instrument. Other stringed instruments include viola, cello and double bass.

Brass for example – trombone
You play it by blowing a raspberry into the mouthpiece (it's true!). You change the note by moving the sliding part of the trombone up and down. Other brass instruments include trumpet, tuba, French horn, euphonium and cornet.

You could also learn the guitar, keyboards, drums or other percussion instruments (like the xylophone). You could even have singing lessons!

People use instruments and voices to praise God, too. Read Psalm 150 to find out how.

Challenge **Get some friends together and make some noise to God. It doesn't matter what it sounds like, if you're praising God. He won't mind how good you are!**

Touch

Touch is a very important part of the way God made us. The nerve endings at the end of our fingers and toes and in our hands and feet help us make sense of the world around us. We can tell if something is sharp, rough, smooth, hot or cold without even looking at it!

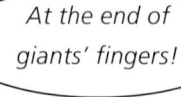

Where do you find giant snails?

At the end of giants' fingers!

Blind people use touch even more than people who can see. They use touch to recognise people, and to read – and that's just two examples.

Challenge Try to recognise your friends by touching their faces.

Blind people can recognise a friend by touching their face. The position and shape of the nose, the eyes and the mouth help them know who the person is. It's not as easy as it sounds. Get a few friends together and try to recognise people just by touching their faces. How difficult is it?

Blind people read through touch by using a special alphabet called Braille. This uses a series of raised dots to form letters and words. Here is the Braille alphabet.

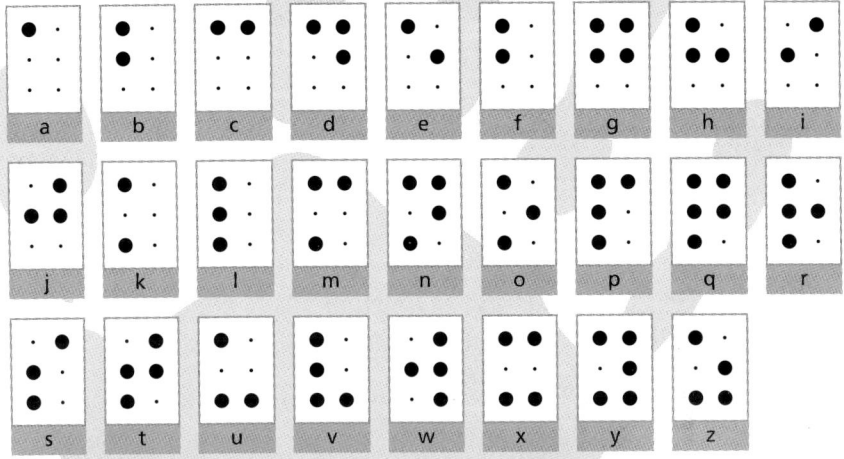

Challenge Write your name in Braille.

Here's what you have to do. On a piece of card, mark out sets of six dots making sure you have enough sets of dots, one for each letter in your name. Get some split pins or raised sticky dots and use those to make the raised dots in each letter. Can your friends "read" what you have "written"? What else can you write in Braille?

Taste

What's your favourite food? Is it sweet (sugary) or savoury (salty or spicy)?

Challenge **Conduct a survey of your mates and family to see what the most popular food is.**

Here are some questions to ask:

1 What is your favourite savoury food?
2 What is your favourite sweet food?
3 Do you prefer sweet or savoury food?
4 What food do you hate the most?
5 If you went to someone's house who then offered you this hated food, would you be polite and eat it?

Challenge **Make some Super-smooth smoooooooooooothies!**

You'll need to use a blender or food processor and maybe a grown-up to help you.

Strawnana Surprise

You will need:
- 1 banana
- 4 strawberries
- 400 ml milk
- 1 tbsp natural yogurt or vanilla ice cream
- Strawberry sauce

Peel the banana and break it up into the blender. Remove the green stalks from the strawberries and add them. Pour in the milk and yogurt/ice cream and blitz the mixture until it is smooth. Pour some strawberry sauce into a glass (not too much, don't go mad!) and then pour the smoothie mixture on top. Enjoy! The surprise comes when you find the thick, tasty strawberry sauce at the end of your yummy smoothie!

The Grapes of Froth

You will need:
- 10 big grapes
- 1 kiwi fruit
- 1 banana
- 3 tbsp yogurt
- 200 ml milk

Prepare all the fruit and place all the ingredients in a blender. Blitz the mixture until smooth. Pour into a glass and guzzle. If the bits of grape skin get annoying, sieve your smoothie before you drink it!

Naughty but Nice

You will need:
- 400 ml chocolate milk
- 15 cherries (with the stones removed)

Once you have taken all the cherry stones out, blitz in the blender with the chocolate milk and enjoy!

Follow the journey of your super smoothies on the next page…

What happened to the kid who drank eight Cokes?

He burped Seven-up!

Your belly

Where does all the food go?

Now you've drunk all the smoothies from the previous page, what happens to them? Opposite is a picture of all the tubes your food goes through when you've eaten it.

Once food has been through your body I think we all know how it comes out again. Your body takes all the good things out of the food to turn it into energy so you can do stuff like play football or dance. When you go to the toilet, that's your body getting rid of all the stuff it can't use.

How clever is that?

If you chew your food properly, it spends about 15 seconds in your **mouth** before you swallow it. Your smoothie will have only spent a second in your mouth!

It only takes a few seconds for your smoothie to go down the **oesophagus** (you say this word o – soph – a – gus), the long tube from your mouth to your stomach.

Food spends up to four hours in your **stomach**. That's why you feel full for a long time if you eat too much food! Your smoothie spends less time there, as the stomach has to do less to break it down.

It can take from one to four hours for food to get through the **small intestine**. This is a tube that is five metres long. Imagine that long a tube wrapped up inside you!

It can take anything up to a couple of days for food to pass through the **large intestine**. Imagine that – food that you ate two days ago might still be inside you!

Eurgh!

Your stuff

Mobiles

Instant communication is what everyone is talking about!

Challenge **Work out these forms of communication.** Answers at the bottom of the page.

CODE CRACKER!

A	☎
B	⌨
C	✉
D	☏
E	⚡
G	✍
H	♟
I	✋
K	🗒
L	✉
M	✎
N	✎
O	▭
P	🖥
R	🖊
S	➤
T	”
X	💬

A mobile phone allows you to...

Play games *Text* *Take pictures* *Talk* *Watch video* *Play music*

What else might a mobile phone let you do in the future? Write your ideas here:

....

....

....

BUT... there are problems with mobile phones.

1 There's still a worry about how using them may affect your health.

2 Sometimes the signal's weak or there's none at all.

3 We have to pay for the calls, games and videos that we use.

4 If you forget to top up or simply can't afford to use it you're stuck!

BUT remember – there is one person we can always talk to. That is God. We said that God loves us and cares for us – pages 10 and 11 if you've forgotten. God talks to us through the Bible but we can also talk to him and listen to him through prayer. We don't need to do anything special to talk to God. And we don't need to top up our "being good" card or be in a place where reception is good! All we have to do is talk and chat to him. He will listen.

Jesus gave us a special prayer to say which covers all the main bits that we might want to say to him.

DID YOU KNOW?

The word "hallowed" means to greatly honour as holy? God is awesome. So we say, "May your name be greatly honoured".

A reminder that we are God's children.

When we belong to God, we are citizens where he is king.

A reminder that God provides us with all we need.

Our **Father** in heaven,
hallowed be your name,
your **kingdom** come,
your will be done,
on earth as in heaven.
Give us today our daily **bread.**
Forgive us our sins
as we forgive those who sin
against us.
Lead us not into temptation
but deliver us from **evil.**
For the kingdom, the power
and the glory are yours,
now and for ever.
Amen

Asking God to sort out the wrong we have done and others have done.

We need God's protection, and we trust him to look after us.

Computers and games

Hard to believe but not long before you were born, computers and chips (not the ones from the chip shop with vinegar!) were very rare. It was only in 1995 that Mr Bill Gates came up with Windows 95 and computers in the home became a lot more common. Since then, the popularity of computers has been huge. Computers and silicon chips are everywhere – from cash cards to fridges, car engines to train tickets. They are meant to make our lives easier.

Then there are the computer games. Computers were originally used to help with work-related jobs. But now the ones we have at home are mainly used by you and me to play games. (Do you know how hard it is to write this book when we want to play *Pro Evolution Soccer 6*?)

Many people spend hours and hours playing games. And, of course, there are different types of games...

Challenge Write down your favourite game (or a well-known game) under the different headings below.

Shoot 'em ups	Role-playing	Simulations

Ever wondered how much time you spend on computer games each week?

Challenge **Take a week of your life and add up how many hours each day you spend playing games.**

Day	Sun	Mon	Tue	Wed	Thurs	Fri	Sat	Total
Hours								

Wow! Did it shock you to see how much time you spend?

Do you think you could spend your time doing something else instead? Like homework, playing football with your mates, walking the dog, helping round the house, talking with people and so on? What about all that time spent just sitting down? Don't you think that just sitting in one place staring at a screen is BORING sometimes?

We're not saying you shouldn't spend time at the computer or games console. After all, it's fun. But as we said before, we should all really try to keep our lives in balance so we keep fit and healthy. That means not just sitting down all the time. As you've seen elsewhere in this book there are plenty of other things to get interested in. Can you name some of the things you've read about so far that you might like to do? What other things could you get involved in? Write them in on the side here, for example, music making, skateboarding…

Gadgets

When it comes to gadgets, boys always seem to be interested. It's because of this interest that the phrase "Boys with toys" was used. Next time you go shopping take a look at the different things that

boys and girls look at. You'll find more boys than girls looking at the latest electronic gifts. That isn't to say that girls aren't interested in gadgets but it does seem that more boys than girls take an interest. (And it doesn't change when you get older!)

The problem with gadgets is that they can cost a lot of money. And as we're sure you know, we should be careful about what we do with our money!

Do you get pocket money? Or have you been given money at Christmas or on your birthday? What is the first thing that you think about using your money for?

Challenge If someone gave you £100, what would you spend it on? Write your thoughts here!

If you lived in Africa or the Asian subcontinent and someone gave you £100 your answer would be very different! In the Western world we are very fortunate to have all that we have – enough food, good clothes and great gadgets. But lots of people in the world don't get enough food or even fresh water to drink. The good news is, we can help people who are less fortunate than us. How? By giving some of what we have to them. **Live Aid**, **Comic Relief** and **Children in Need** are all well-known charity events that raise money for those who need help. There are many other charities too.

Tearfund is a relief charity that works with partners to bring help and hope to communities in need around the world. Tearfund believes that young people are the activists for now and in the future.

Visit *The Action Pack* website www.tearfund.org.uk/actionpack to discover stories, games, prayer ideas, recipes and facts, and the Comedy Camel jokes!

Your heart

When people talk about their hearts, they don't always mean the beating thing inside their chests, pumping the blood round their bodies! The heart can also mean the emotions – how you feel. Feelings are really important. We can feel happy, sad, cross, excited... we can love someone, be angry with them... these are all emotions. How do you feel about your mum, your dad or the person who cares for you? How do you feel about your mates, your dog, your cat, your favourite football team? We've already talked about self-image and how you feel about yourself. We're going to think some more about that now.

Just average?

John was just an average boy. He wasn't very good at anything, but he wasn't very bad at anything either. If you had to describe him you'd say he was simply ordinary – played a little football, had a few friends, never got into much trouble. He was simply an ordinary and average lad.

Sometimes, being ordinary and average troubled him.

"Why can't I be good at anything?" he asked his mum.

"John, you *are* good at things," she replied, lovingly.

"I'm good at a few things, but I'm not great at anything," John grumbled. "I want to be great at something, to be noticed by people. Ordinary is boring."

John often talked like this with his mum. In his heart he longed for people to really notice him. He was in the football team at school, but usually as a substitute. He wasn't one of the great players, not like Kyle. Kyle was a brilliant player. He wasn't average. Everyone liked Kyle and that was because he wasn't ordinary and average. Kyle was everything John wanted to be.

Kyle had great hair. Kyle had the latest games for his console. Kyle even had a girlfriend (although John wasn't interested in girls and the thought of having one was horrible!). Kyle always had the latest clothes. He had a fantastic BMX and the hottest skateboard money could buy.

John felt fed up about being ordinary for months and months.

His school team had made it to the cup final. Once again, because he was good but not that good, John was a substitute. It was an exciting game but there was no score. John's team were playing well, but so were the other team.

And then it happened – Kyle scored… a typical, fantastic goal. He dribbled past a couple of defenders and struck the ball so hard that it shot past the goalkeeper. Kyle didn't do ordinary. The crowd cheered and everyone watching had to admit that this was an amazing goal.

All through the second half John's team, even with Kyle playing, couldn't score another goal. It remained 1–0. Then, as the match neared its end, disaster struck for John's team. The other side scored an equaliser. It was 1–1. If it stayed this way the cup would be decided on penalties.

But there was one more disaster for John's team. With two minutes to go, Kyle was doing his best to score a winner. After all, he was the best player on the pitch and if anyone could score it would be him. He made one last desperate run at the defence, flicked the ball to the left and was just about to take a shot when he skidded to the ground.

Everyone in the crowd gasped, including John. Kyle didn't jump up as usual. He lay on the ground with his leg at an awkward angle. He was in agony. He wouldn't be playing any more today. This was desperate news for John's team with a penalty shoot-out almost inevitable. Kyle, obviously, was the best penalty taker in John's school. He never missed.

The PE teacher and team

manager came up to John. "OK, John," he said, "Kyle won't be able to play. Tie your boots up and get out there. You may need to have a shot at a penalty!"

"Y... y... yes, sir!" John replied, feeling a bit nervous at the thought.

He pulled off his track bottoms, tied up his boots and ran out onto the pitch. The match restarted and, just as the ball was going to be passed to John, the referee blew the final whistle.

It was now down to penalties.

John was only average at taking penalties so his name wasn't very high on the list of takers but it was there. He hoped the competition was finished before he had to take his.

First of all, each team would take it in turn to score the best out of five penalties. If there were still no clear winner after that, there would be a sudden-death penalty.

The penalty competition started. After each team had attempted to score five goals, the score was 2–2. No clear winner. So they went into sudden death.

John was the third person on this list. He hoped that it would all be over before he had to go. He wasn't that good at penalties, after all.

After two more attempts by both teams the score was 3–3. So it was John's turn. The boy from the other team stepped up and took his penalty. The ball soared over the goal and missed. Still 3–3 and if John scored, his team would win the cup.

John stepped up and placed the ball on the penalty spot. He took a few steps back. He knew he wasn't very good at penalties and as he looked at the goal it looked really small and the goalkeeper looked really large. John felt sick inside and weak in his legs. He was just average and ordinary. To score a penalty you needed to be special and super-skilful... you needed to be someone like Kyle.

John closed his eyes and concentrated. He would run up, kick the ball into the left corner of the goal and hope for the best. He opened his eyes, ran up and kicked the ball...

GOAL!

John's team had won the cup because of his penalty. It had been a good penalty kick and the ball had gone into the left corner while the goalkeeper dived the other way.

After the match, the school team celebrated. Kyle hobbled up to John, leaning on crutches, his ankle in a bandage.

"Are you OK, Kyle?" John asked.

"Yeah, it's just sprained, " Kyle said. "I should be playing again in a few weeks. But I don't want to talk about my ankle. I came over to say well done. That was a great penalty kick. You hit the ball perfectly. I normally fluff my penalties. I never know what I'm going to do. I just run up and hit them. But you looked totally in control. It was great. You know what, John? You are a great penalty taker. Sometimes I wish I were like you."

John wasn't sure what to say or do. He had thought he was simply ordinary, average, not particularly good or bad, simply John. But here was Kyle, the great Kyle wishing that he were like John! Wow...

John wasn't average or ordinary. No person on the planet is ordinary and average. We are all different and wonderful. We can all do some of the things we think we can't do – and we can often surprise others with what we can do! But don't be too amazed if others think more highly of you than you think of yourself.

Remember: you are not ordinary or average. You are a unique person who God loves and cares for. And you've got unique talents and gifts. So feel good about yourself today! We dare you to shout out at the top of your voice:

"I FEEL GooD ABouT MYSELF toDAY!"

Doing what's right

This is a serious subject but we're going to have some fun.

Challenge Try this fun quiz to see what sort of person you are.

1 You see an old lady struggling with some shopping. Do you...

(a) Laugh and be glad that you aren't old and frail like her ☐

(b) Go to help but then remember that *Dr Who* is on TV so rush home ☐

(c) Offer to carry her bags and then make her some cocoa when you get to her house? ☐

2 Your friend needs a pound to get home as he has lost his money. Do you...

(a) Wave to him as you get on the bus to go home ☐

(b) Explain that you would give him some money but you are saving it for a rainy day ☐

(c) Give him the pound you were saving for some chips on the way home? ☐

3 You see some younger boys bullying another kid. Do you...

(a) Join in – you like a bit of exercise ☐

(b) Pretend you don't see what's happening and clear off ☐

(c) Find a teacher to help (at school) or go over and help the victim (if out of school)? ☐

4 Your mum needs some help cleaning the house. Do you...

(a) Leg it ☐

(b) Say that you would help but your teeth are itchy today ☐

(c) Make her a cup of tea and tell her to sit down and watch a movie while you do it all? ☐

5 Your homework is due in today but you haven't done it. Do you...

(a) Find the smallest kid in the class and take his homework, hand it in and say it's your own ☐

(b) Find a friend and copy their homework very quickly and hand it in ☐

(c) Own up that you have forgotten to do the work and ask the teacher if you can do it tonight? ☐

Now you can see what sort of person you are. Look at the results of this highly accurate and scientific test...(!)

If you answered mostly a's: Aargh! You're not very nice at all, are you? Ever thought about changing your attitude?

Mostly b's: Hmm... room for improvement! You aren't bad on the outside but deep down, we think you only really care about yourself!

Mostly c's: You are too good to be true! (And if you got all c's, are you being really honest? No one is that good and nice all the time – not even us, the authors!)

More rights and wrongs

That was a fun quiz and you shouldn't take the results too seriously! But let's take a quick look at who and what influences us to act in the way that we do.

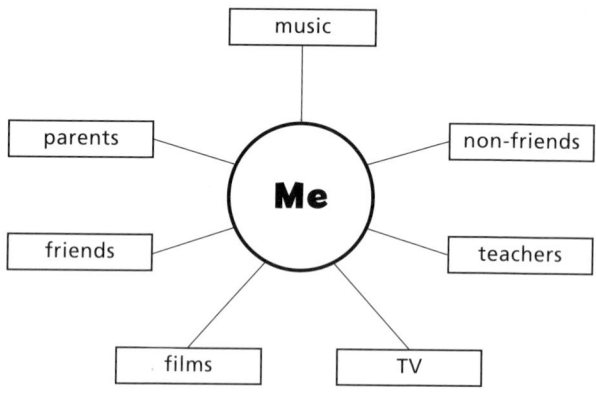

Challenge Is there anything missing that influences you?

There are probably many more influences on the way we live than those listed above. Are there any in your life that you can think of?

....

....

....

....

....

....

....

All these things help shape the way we act and the decisions we make.

However, there is someone even more important who can help us make decisions. God made us, cares for us and wants the best for us. So it's not surprising that he should be able to help us the most. Take a look at the new diagram.

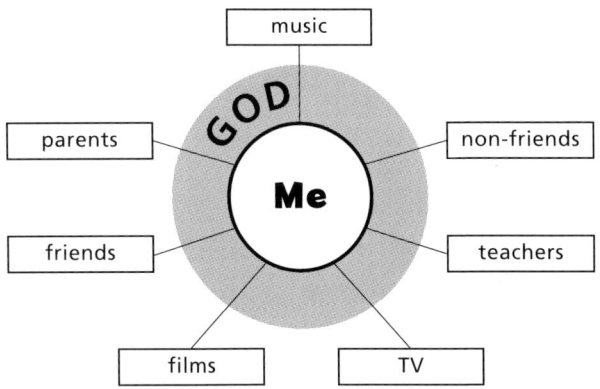

With all your heart you must trust the LORD
  and not your own judgment.
Always let him lead you,
  and he will clear the road for you to follow.

Proverbs 3:5–6

If you want to know more about how God can help YOU, talk to a friend or relative or even a teacher you know is a Christian. You might belong to a church, and could talk to someone there, or to the person who gave you **NO GIRLS ALLOWED!** You can also read the Bible. (If you haven't got a Bible, maybe you could ask someone to buy you one.) To help you with this, look back to page 59 to see how *Snapshots* can help you hear from God.

Your past and your future

Family trees

Where do you come from? No, we don't mean which town or city were you born in, or where you live! Who are your family? What do they look like? All families are different. Even in the Bible there were some pretty weird families. You heard of Joseph? His story is in Genesis, the first book of the Bible. His dad had two wives at the same time (yes, two!) and two women who he treated like wives (crazy!), and Joseph had 11 brothers and at least one sister. Imagine having all those annoying brothers! They were a bad lot because they sold Joseph as a slave because they didn't like him. A bit extreme!

Joseph's family tree would have looked like this:

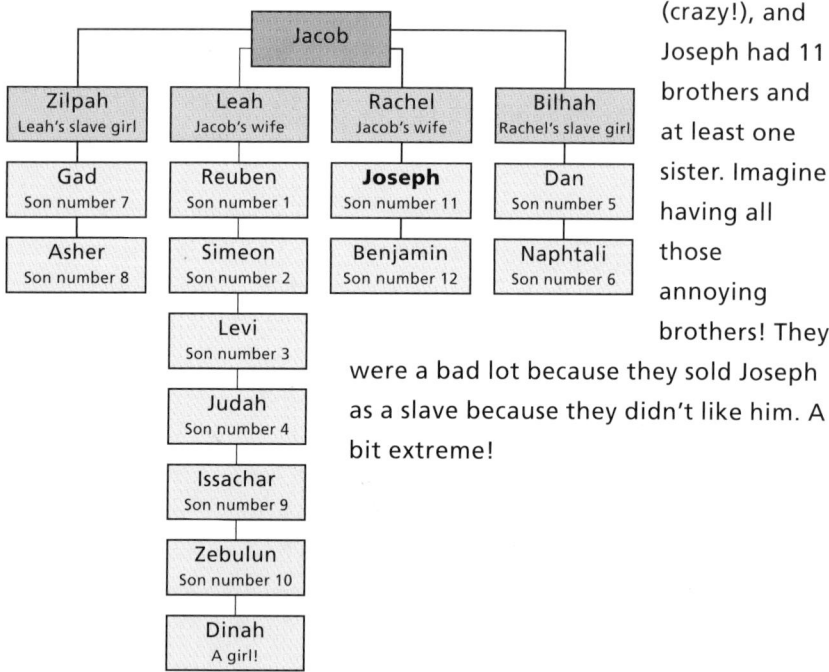

Jacob

Zilpah	Leah	Rachel	Bilhah
Leah's slave girl	Jacob's wife	Jacob's wife	Rachel's slave girl
Gad	Reuben	**Joseph**	Dan
Son number 7	Son number 1	Son number 11	Son number 5
Asher	Simeon	Benjamin	Naphtali
Son number 8	Son number 2	Son number 12	Son number 6
	Levi		
	Son number 3		
	Judah		
	Son number 4		
	Issachar		
	Son number 9		
	Zebulun		
	Son number 10		
	Dinah		
	A girl!		

Can you see why it's called a family tree? It starts small and then branches out!

What would your family tree look like? Would it be as complicated as Joseph's?

Challenge **Try writing down your family tree in the space below.**

Ask your mum, dad or the person who looks after you to help you. Start by putting your name in the box below.

Farmer John "That pig is like one of the family."

Farmer Bob "Really? Which one?"

Psst: Sometimes families are a lot like Joseph's, with arguments and separations. If people around you don't want to talk about your family tree, leave this activity and try another page in the book.

What do you want to be?

Some people have wanted to do one thing ever since they can remember, but others change their mind every year. To give you some idea of what jobs some people do and why they might do them, we interviewed five people and asked them three questions:

- **What's the best thing about your job?**
- **What's the worst thing about your job?**
- **Why did you decide to do your job?**

Here's what they said!

Dan

Works with people with special needs

- **Best**: Seeing people do things they've never done before.
- **Worst**: When people don't work together as a team.
- **Why**: I fell into it by accident!

Tash

A singer

- **Best thing**: I just love singing. Sometimes it doesn't seem like work and I get to meet interesting people!
- **Worst**: Being ill – if I'm ill with a cold or sore throat, I can't work.
- **Why**: It's all I ever wanted to do – it was my biggest dream. Someone's got to be a singer – why not me?

Dave

A paramedic

- **Best**: Being able to help people.
- **Worst**: Driving to the scene of a motorway pileup.
- **Why**: I like food, science and people. I get to work with all three in this job!

Challenge What about you? What will you be doing when you're grown up? Think about what you'd really like to do and then imagine we interviewed YOU about your job. Could you answer the same questions as the people here? Have a guess...

Name

Job

• **Best**:

• **Worst**:

• **Why**:

Steve

Works for a charity that helps people who don't have enough

• **Best**: Travelling and working with people from other countries.
• **Worst**: Having an inbox full of emails that need to be answered when I get back to the office!
• **Why**: I met a woman in Kenya who had to choose which of her children she would let die. She didn't have enough food to feed them all. I wanted to help people like her, so that they never had to make that choice.

Alan

Works with computers

• **Best**: Solving hundreds of problems and bringing order out of chaos!
• **Worst**: When you're let down by other people who are meant to be doing work for you.
• **Why**: I enjoy problem-solving!

Where do you want to go?

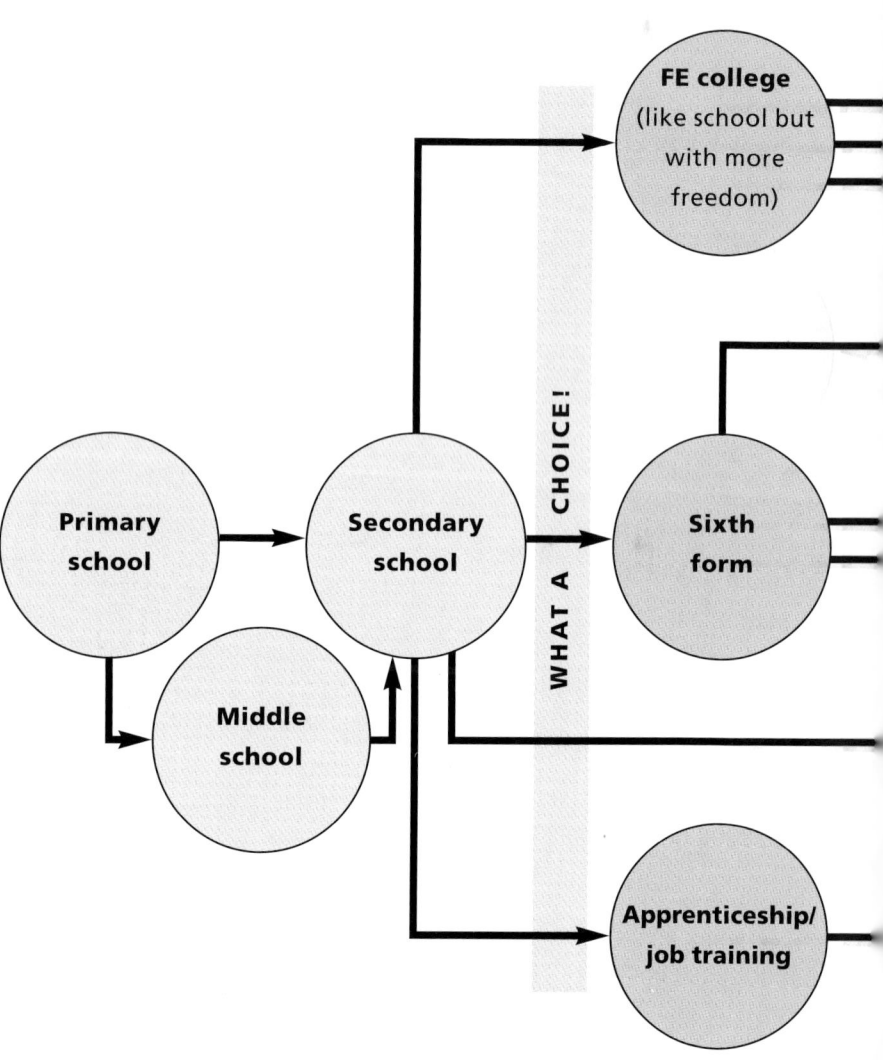

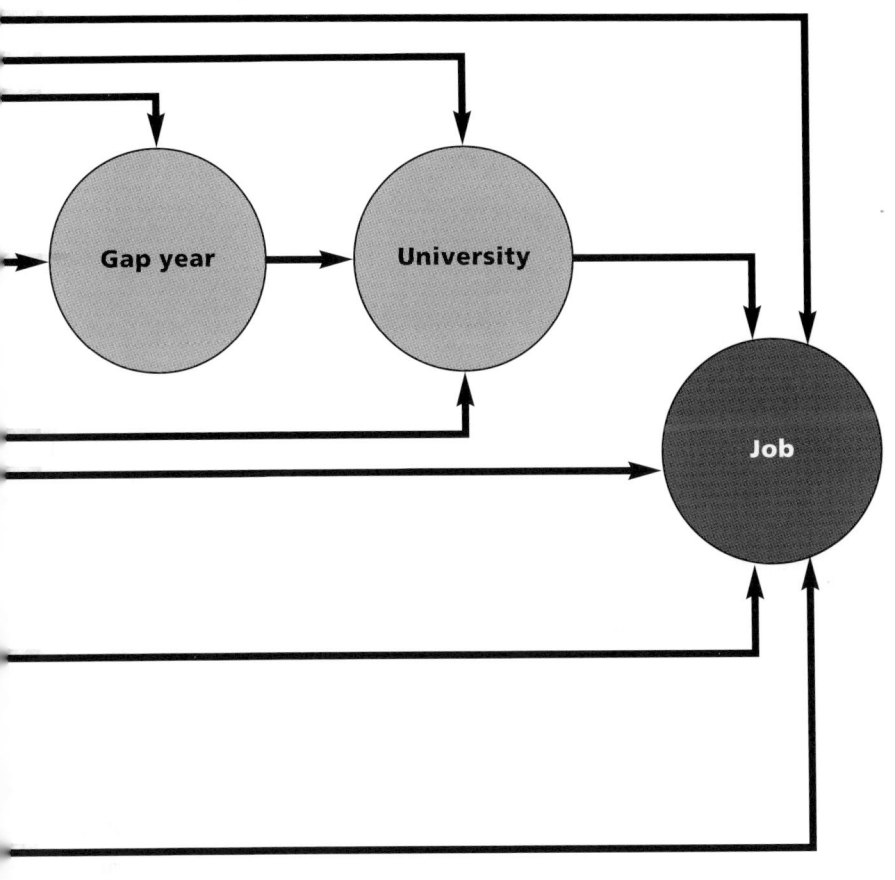

God and your future

Thinking about the future can be scary, or it can be exciting! What would you think if you were asked the question, "What will you be doing in 30 years' time?" You'll have a lot of choices to make before then. The chart on pages 88 and 89 shows just how many choices there will be even before you reach the age of 18!

However, one thing is certain:

God is with you and is interested in every choice you make.

He wants to help you make all the difficult decisions. Look at some of the people in the Bible who asked God for help with their futures.

What does God say he did before Jeremiah was born?

What does Jeremiah say?

What does God promise Jeremiah?

Challenge
Read these verses from Jeremiah 1:4–8, and look out for the answers to the questions in the speech bubbles.

The LORD said:
"Jeremiah, I am your Creator,
and before you were born,
I chose you to speak for me
to the nations."
I (Jeremiah) replied, "I'm not a good speaker,
LORD, and I'm too young."
"Don't say you're too young," the LORD
answered. "If I tell you to go and speak to
someone, then go! And when I tell you what to
say, don't leave out a word! I promise to be
with you and keep you safe, so don't be afraid."

God had asked Jeremiah to do something really tough because the people he was going to talk to (from Israel) would not want to listen to him. Jeremiah says he is too young but God would not accept that as an excuse. He has chosen Jeremiah to do this job and would give him the words to say. If sometimes you feel you are too young to think about what God wants you to do, remember the encouragement God gave to Jeremiah.

Copy and then decorate this "Learn and remember" verse and stick it somewhere you can see it. Try to remember it too. While you decorate it, chat to God about what you would like to do in the future and ask him to be with you.

Psst: Now you've come to the end of **NO GIRLS ALLOWED!** *look back at the bits you've liked doing. Maybe there are things you haven't done yet. Have you enjoyed this book? Give it marks out of ten here*

I promise to be with you and keep you safe, so don't be afraid.

Jeremiah 1:8

/10

Your notes

A man goes into a butcher's shop.

"Can you give me some bits for my dog?" he asks.

"Certainly, sir," said the butcher, "which bits is he missing?"

Note to me!!
Read my Bible on my own.
Find out about *Snapshots*, Scripture
Union's Bible Guide for people like me.
www.scriptureunion.org.uk/snapshots

What do you get if you cross a skeleton and a dog?

An animal that buries itself in the garden!

Answers

Pages 20–21
The total number of squares is 55.

Pages 22–23
Missing letters
J, J and O. The letters represent the first letter of each month of the year.

Grid

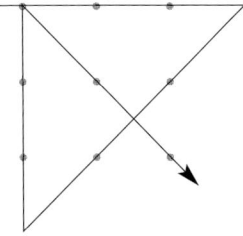

Missing word
The missing word is Sleepy, one of the seven dwarfs!

Pages 24–25
Link words
BACK**PACK**AGE
HUMAN**KIND**NESS
FOOT**HOLD**FAST

Wordsearch

Pages 26–27
Spot the difference

Pages 38–39
Cricket positions
Silly mid-leg
Long backward-cover
Middle leg
Forward round spike
Way long off
Bad leg
Wally
Right on
Right off
Last slip

Books

Parabulz

Andrew Bianchi and Andy Gray

Stories told by Jesus, Ezekiel, Nathan and others get a new treatment in this zany book written by Andrew Bianchi and illustrated by Andy Gray. You'll laugh, be puzzled, but beware! You may find yourself trapped by a Gotcha! A must-read for all readers of **NO GIRLS ALLOWED!**

Massive Prayer Adventure

Sarah Mayers

Make a fresh start in the way you talk with God. Discover loads about him and try out different ways of speaking and listening. You are in for a surprise! Another must-read!

Psst: **Friends Forever!** is like **NO GIRLS ALLOWED!** Try that too, but beware! All your girlfriends may have got there first! "Girlfriends!" did we hear you yell? Well, let's just say, people in your class or group who happen not to be boys!

For more details visit www.scriptureunion.org.u